Journey Into Reality

Through Prayer and God-Centeredness

by

Joann Nesser

LIVING WATERS PUBLISHING

Journey Into Reality

published by
Living Waters Publishing

International Standard Book Number:
0-9659320-4-4

Living Waters Publishing
15590 Highland Ave. N.W.
Prior Lake, MN 55372
Toll-free: 888-950-2772
http://www.livingwaterspublishing.com

Printed in the United States of America

Publisher's Cataloging-in-Publication
(Provided by Quality Books, Inc.)

Nesser, Joann.
Journey into reality : through prayer and God-centeredness / Joann Nesser. -- 1st ed.
p. cm.
ISBN: 0-9659320-4-4

1. Prayer--Christianity. 2. Spiritual life--Christianity.
3. God--Worship and love. I. Title.

BV215.N47 1998 248.32
QBI98-283

Introduction

Many years ago, when I was searching for a meaningful relationship with God through prayer, the classics of devotional literature became my mentors—and were very helpful for my spiritual growth. As my relationship with the Creator evolved, I became concerned about the spiritual legacy this generation would leave for those who follow in the footsteps of our faith.

It seems to me that many Christians of our generation have a shallow experience of God and, because of our culture, have more of a rational, scientific faith. They seem to be starving to death for lack of prayer. God began to give me a desire to share what I had learned about prayer in my quest and through my mentors.

When I was first asked to lead a retreat on prayer, some of this desire to share with the Church was fulfilled. However, it seemed that many more people could be reached through books. I felt that someday I would try to write what God had shown me, limited as it might be. So far, I have never been able to find the extended quiet time one needs to write. A friend suggested transcribing retreat sessions for publication. The idea excited me. I have no illusions that this fits the classic devotional status, but I pray it will be meaningful to you nonetheless.

These particular little talks, entitled *"Journey into Reality,"* was given as a retreat to persons who had already begun seeking a deeper prayer life. My intention was to remind them that prayer is not an escape from reality but a journey into reality.

Joann Nesser

To reach Joann Nesser, please write or call:

Christos Center for Spiritual Formation
1212 Holly Drive
Lino Lakes, MN 55038
612/653-8207

Table of Contents

Retreat into Silence

Why do we go on retreat? Is it a time to get away from family, traffic, work or some other "problem"? Why do we go? We should go simply to meet with God. This is why we go out into the "wilderness", why we go on retreat. We follow the tradition of our ancestors—who went into the desert to renew themselves and meet God.

We retreat for a time of solitude and silence, to be apart from the world and close to God. Oftentimes, we will meet our adversary, too—the one who would like to stand in the way of God's intentions. And, oftentimes, we will meet our true self. We retreat to place ourselves in a position to receive what God gives. It is an intentional "setting ourselves apart" to listen, to have no agenda of our own, to simply be open to God. It is being vulnerable to God, disallowing distractions and allowing God time to work in a significant way in our hearts.

On retreat, we do not have to pay attention to others. We do not have to make small talk. We do not have to be something for somebody else. We go there to be open to God. Even if we have no idea what God wants to do, or why, even if we do not think God really needs to do any major work—we can still retreat. We do not have to go because we have some crisis which needs fixing. We go because we want to know God, to say, "Here I am, God, do what you want." I believe God takes a life and does something just because we present ourselves.

I like to read devotional literature because it stirs up my passion for God. It stirs up the possibilities of what God can do with my life. I like biographies and autobiographies, books written about someone's life, or by someone about their own spiritual journey. The reason I like them is because they show me what God can do with a life that is surrendered. They give me courage and the impetus to surrender. They make me desire to give myself to God.

I like to read about great saints and great Christians of the past, because I learn about ordinary persons through whom God did extraordinary things. If God could do extraordinary things through them, then God can do something with my life! It does not matter how ordinary I am, or how weak I am, or how many times I have failed. Think about the life of one of the great saints in scripture. If God could do something with David, couldn't God do something with you? We can learn something from another's experience; for example, no sin is too great for God to overcome.

The following quote is from Sadhu Sundar Singh, the great Indian Christian mystic. He says something so wonderful about why we go on retreat, why we go away to be with God in an intentional way, why we go to dwell in the wilderness, why we go dwell on the mountaintop:

> "On the mountains, torrents flow right along cutting their own courses, but on the plains, canals have to be dug out painfully by men so that the water might flow. So among those who live on the heights with God, the Holy Spirit makes its way through of its own accord, whereas those who devote little time to prayer and communion with God have to organize painfully."

What a wonderful quote! We need to spend time with God. Never is this time wasted. Never are we giving God too much time. Never are we losing something because we're giving time to God. Never.

We need to spend time dwelling on the heights. It is okay to say it! I can say, "I want to be on the heights with God! I want to be there! I want to be a Sadhu Sundar Singh! I want to be like him!" Paul says, "Imitate me as I imitate Christ." We can say, "I want to imitate Paul. I want to imitate David. I want to imitate Deborah. I want to imitate Teresa of Avila. I want to place myself in a position where God can work in me. I do not want to leave any stone unturned in becoming the person God created me to be."

If we would give adequate time to God, we would spend our life much more simply. If we nurtured our inner life and deep union with God, we would find all of life so much easier, so much less complicated. Many great writers on prayer say prayer becomes more simple as one grows in maturity. The Christian life becomes simpler. Everything simplifies when you grow in your relationship with God. If we picture what our true purpose is, we will give adequate time to God. We won't think it is unusual to retreat to be with God.

Sometimes we get things altogether backward. We try to "make time" for prayer. We try to "set some time aside"so we can be with God. If we really knew, if we REALLY understood why we were created and what life is all about, we would give time with God first priority. Our relationship with God would be the center of our life. Our main purpose would be to be with God. All the other things we do—like work, leisure, service—would "fit in" around our relationship with God. We are created for that relationship.

The Westminster Catechism states that *". . . the*

chief end of (humankind) is to love God and enjoy Him forever. " Isn't it simple?

In the book, Practicing His Presence, Frank Laubach wrote about an experiment he tried after fifteen years of being a minister, a missionary, and a writer. In his experiment, Laubach tried to set his thoughts on God all day long. He wrote:

> "But why do I constantly harp upon this inner experience? Because I feel convinced that for me and for you who read, there lie ahead undiscovered continents of spiritual living compared with which we are infants in arms. And I must witness that people outside are treating me differently. Obstacles which I once would have regarded as insurmountable are melting away like a mirage. People are becoming friendlier who suspected or neglected me before. I feel like one who has had his violin out of tune with the orchestra and at last is in harmony with the universe. As for me, I never lived, I was half dead, I was a rotting tree until I reached the place where I wholly with utter honesty resolved and then re-resolved that I would find God's will and would do that will though every fiber in me said no, and I would win the battle in my thoughts. It was as though some deep artesian well had been struck in my soul of souls and strength came forth."

Laubach experienced a change of life. Why? He goes on to say,

> "I do not claim success even for a day yet, not complete success all day, but some days are close to success and every day is tingling with the joy of a glorious discovery. That

> thing is eternal, that thing is undefeatable. You and I shall soon blow away from our bodies. Money, praise, poverty, opposition, these make no difference, for they will all alike be forgotten in a thousand years, but this Spirit which comes to a mind set upon continuous surrender, this Spirit is timeless life."

We need to learn to nurture the inner life because it is Life. We are penny wise and pound foolish when it comes to spiritual things. "I do not have time for prayer," say the people who need it the most. "Oh, I could not go for a weekend without talking. I would never make it." Yet they are the ones who would most benefit from it .

We waste our life away. Yet God is the very center, the very life, the very heart of life. Jesus says in John 14:6, *"I am the way, and the truth, and the life."* He says in John 10:10, *"I came that they may have life, and have it abundantly."* This is why we retreat, to have time for God, to be vulnerable and open, allowing God to do deep surgery which could not be done in other ways without the quiet space and time.

Scriptures for Meditation:
John 14:13-21
John 15:7-9

Lord, teach us to pray. Bring us into the reality of your abiding presence.

Separation

The theme for this book is "Journey into Reality." Spiritual life is a journey. Pilgrim's Progress by John Bunyan is a classic example of the journey. It's the story of the Christian pilgrim on his or her journey, growing to maturity. Another great example is Bernard Christenson's book, Inward Pilgrimage. The spiritual life is a journey, it is a pilgrimage. It is a journey from brokenness to wholeness, a journey from sinfulness to holiness. It is a journey from a state of separation from God to a state of union with God. We are growing, changing, and deepening. We are broadening. We are becoming more and more like Christ. We move from one degree of glory to another, as II Corinthians 3:18 states:

> *"And all of us, with unveiled faces, seeing the glory of the Lord as though reflected in a mirror, are being transformed into the same image from one degree of glory to another; for this comes from the Lord, the Spirit."*

The goal of this journey is the very image of Jesus himself. He desires us to be like him. We could say it is a journey from a lie to the truth. We could say it is a journey from a false reality to THE TRUE REALITY. We could say it is a journey from who I thought I was to who I really am—who God intends me to be. Scripture tells us we are created in the image of God. In the book of Genesis God said, *"Let us make humankind in our image, according to our likeness. . . ."* We were created to have perfect fellowship with God, to have a perfect relationship. We were created in the image of God, and through sin the relationship has been broken. →

God created us to be available for perfect friendship with our Creator. Think about this friendship. Think about the Garden of Eden. Think of Eden, of Adam and Eve, and how they actually walked with God in the garden. It must have been a perfect climate, wouldn't you guess? It must have been like Hawaii, only a little cooler, beautiful and lush and green, with no mosquitoes. It was perfect, so nothing would hinder Adam and Eve's relationship with God and with one another.

God often walked in the garden with them, for in Genesis 3:8 we read, *"They heard the sound of the Lord God walking in the garden at the time of the evening breeze, and the man and his wife hid themselves from the presence of the Lord God among the trees of the garden."* Because they had sinned, they hid themselves from God. We read, *" . . . (They) hid themselves from the presence of the Lord God among the trees of the garden."* Doesn't this make you sad?

Think of how we long to know God's presence. Isn't this the search of our life? Isn't this what we hunger for? We go to prayer meetings. We go to church. We worship. We do all these things; and what is our favorite part? It is when God's presence is truly felt, when God feels very near. We are so grateful for a little taste of God's presence, just a little bit. Adam and Eve experienced that. They walked in the garden with God. Then they hid themselves. They lost the very thing for which we hunger, and for which we long, crave and desire, the thing which makes us know that we are loved and blessed by God: God's presence. Psalm 16:11 says, *". . . In your presence there is fullness of joy. . . ."*

When we think we have lost God's presence, we question: What have I done? Is there something wrong with me when I go through a dry time, a desert, wilderness time? We want to be in God's presence all the time. Adam and Eve hid themselves. But God's intention was for them to experience their Creator's presence and to have fullness of joy—and this is God's intention for us. God is renewing, transforming, and recreating us so we can experience the fullness of joy for which we were created. This is what scripture says. This is what it is all about.

Genesis 3:8 says that they hid themselves. Before sin they were not conscious of themselves. God said, *"Who told you that you were naked?"* Before sin they did not even know their nakedness.

They were innocent, like little children. Have you ever watched little ones when you are trying to get them ready for bed? They run around the house totally stark-naked, and they could care less. They do not even think about it. Everybody thinks they are cute because they are so uninhibited. They are un-selfconscious. They are totally abandoned. They do not even think about the fact that they are naked. God's question was an acknowledgment: *"Who told you that you were naked?"*

Isn't it sad when little children begin to grow up? I hated it when my children lost that innocence. I hated it when they became self-conscious. For many years our youngest son thought that the whole world loved him. It never crossed his mind that someone didn't think he was wonderful. He would walk up to a total stranger and say, "Will you tie my shoe?" He had no fear of adults and he had many friends. I hated it when he started first grade and we had to start telling him, "Don't talk to strangers. Don't accept candy from anyone." The first time someone calls your child "you stupid so-and-so," he or she starts getting wounded. Soon they start getting shy and self-conscious and afraid of people. They begin to worry that people are not going to like the way they dress, look, or act.

In the beginning, Adam and Eve were innocent. They were totally selfless in attitude. They enjoyed God's presence. Then God said, *"Who told you that you were naked?"* Our sinfulness is our self-consciousness, our self-centeredness, our woundedness, our brokenness. Every single person alive suffers from rejection. We suffer it not so much because of all the rejection we have experienced from one another, but because of the state of our relationship with God. How do you think Adam and Eve felt when they had to hide themselves? I am sure the feeling was one of rejection, even though they caused the problem themselves. That is why we feel as we do—rejected or separated.

As we grow in our union with God and come back to our "Eden", we begin to lose the feeling of rejection because we are no longer separated. We come out of a state of sinfulness, of self-centeredness, of low self-image, of rejection, and of pain. We are growing and being transformed into the image of Christ, the true Son of God, the perfect manifestation of what God intends us to be. It is as if God says, "Here is a picture of what I intend you to be." If we look at scripture, we see in Romans 8:29 that Jesus was to be the firstborn of many: *"For those whom he foreknew he also predestined to be conformed to the image of his Son, in order that he might be the firstborn within a large family."*

Jesus is our example, he is the first one of us. We are to be like Jesus—this is our journey. Jesus is the image of God, God incarnate in human flesh, and we are to return to the image of God (as originally created), to the image of Jesus Christ. That which we came from—brokenness, self-centeredness, rejection, fragmentation—is unreality. It is the lie. But Jesus has redeemed us and is bringing us to reality, to what we are intended to be, to the reason for our creation. That sinful self—that is unreality. The person God intends us to be—that is reality. We are created for that reality.

God is so immense. God's *"Godness"* is so infinite and so many-faceted that every person can fit in. Every person can be fully his or her self. He or she can be fully, completely unique and different from any other person and still be fully the image of God—because God's character, God's personality, is so infinite.

Have you ever heard someone say Jesus had all the gifts of the Holy Spirit, but we can't have all the gifts because we are not Jesus? Or, have you heard someone say God's character is full of compassion, mercy, love, all of these things, but we cannot possibly hope for that level of perfection? Scripture says we are to become like Christ. Scripture also says that all of God's glorious personality can be manifested through the human life, as long as there is surrender, healing and wholeness.

Of course, we will never be perfectly like Jesus because we dwell in human flesh. It is the surrender, the intention, the desire of our heart to be like Jesus that God really wants. Teresa of Avila is quoted as saying, "To the degree that we seek Him we will find Him." The desire of our heart is where God works, not in our ability to fulfill the desire. Our role is to surrender. God becomes the light shining out of the darkness, the treasure in the earthen vessel.

We are drawn out of unreality, into our Creator and to reality. This journey is one of becoming like Christ. We allow God to work this transformation in us by beholding the glory of God, by loving God.

We have no greater work than to get to know God. How can we become the image of Jesus? The work is done by the Holy Spirit. Our role is to present ourselves to God. Our role is to say, "Here I am! Do it! I want all you've got! I want to be everything you want me to be. I want you to take my life and do everything you can with it. Where I am not surrendered, make me surrendered. Show me. Work in me!" If I am to become the image of Christ then I must focus on God, not look at myself!

Usually, we look at ourselves and try to root out some little flaw, train some part of our character that is not the way it should be—or we try to act holier than the rest and do all the "right" things. We try to reach God by self effort.

But II Corinthians 3:18 says,

> *"And all of us, with unveiled faces, seeing the glory of the Lord as though reflected in a mirror, are being transformed into the same image from one degree of glory to another; for this comes from the Lord, the Spirit."*

We behold God's glory and are being transformed into Jesus' image. This comes from God. Instead of being self-focused and self-centered, we can focus on God. This is our role. God's role is to be the one to change us. This is our quest—to allow God to change us. Our goal is to forget all about self, forget about sins, flaws in character and failures. We must forget about them. What we have done wrong yesterday, the day before and the day after, forget. WE cannot change our past mistakes. We can ask for forgiveness, but we cannot go back and undo our mistakes, so we might as well forget them. Remembering past mistakes will only be a weight about our necks which will keep us from being able to follow Christ. We must forget. We must take our eyes off ourselves and focus on God.

Dom Hubert Von Zeller says in one of his

writings, "Meditation is to prayer what study is to wisdom." Traditionally, people of prayer have meditated on scripture as they learn to focus on God. If we want to fully enter into a deep interior life and be fully present so God can work in us, we need to learn to be meditators on the Word of God.

Scriptures for Meditation:
Genesis 1:26-31,
Genesis 3:8-11,
Isaiah 43:1-7,
II Corinthians 3:18,
John 3:16-17, 10:10,
Romans 8:29,
John 14:6

Look deeply at these verses, and let them form in your imagination and in your inner being. Expect God to say something new and rich to you.

Creator God, we pray that you will enlarge our understanding, that you will enlighten the eyes of our hearts, that you will go beyond our human wisdom and our fragmented, broken, self-conscious selves and speak reality and truth to our inner person. We pray we can grow up to the image of God, the fullness of Christ. Let us be a manifestation of your Son to a lost and hurting world, we pray in Jesus' name. Amen.

Transformation

We were originally created in God's image, and our spiritual journey is a return to this image. God's intention for us is that we become the full image of Christ. One reason God sent Christ was to say, "See, this is what you can be like, this is what you were created to be." God says, "This is your example of God dwelling in human flesh." Jesus is our brother, the firstborn of a large family.

Jesus is our perfect example. Of course, we know that because of our human nature, we will never be sinless in this life. But we must strive to allow God to work through us, to allow the Holy Spirit to create Christ in us. Our whole spiritual journey is Christ forming himself in us. In Romans 8:9-11 we read:

> *"But you are not in the flesh; you are in the Spirit, since the Spirit of God dwells in you. Anyone who does not have the Spirit of Christ does not belong to him. But if Christ is in you, though the body is dead because of sin, the Spirit is life because of righteousness. If the Spirit of him who raised Jesus from the dead dwells in you, he who raised Christ from the dead will give life to your mortal bodies also through his Spirit that dwells in you."*

We talk about this as a journey. We are being taken on this journey from a state of fragmentation to a state of wholeness, from the lie of who we thought we were to the truth of who we are to become, from unreality to reality. This is a journey of healing the broken, separated and rejected, bringing us to union and oneness. Have you ever heard people talking about the atonement as the *at-one-ment*? God is taking us to oneness, from a broken nature to wholeness. We are journeying to the manifestation of the image of Jesus.

Externally, the journey is not apparent. The journey is the transformation taking place within. The treasure is in the earthen vessel. The light shines out of the darkness. The light comes from inside this earthen vessel. Your appearance will not change, you will not suddenly look holy. It is not an external kind of manifestation. It is the treasure in the earthen vessel that shines forth and makes the transformation. It is not by our outward acts so much as by our inward yielding that the journey takes place.

Very naturally, because of this inward transformation, the outward acts begin to change. Teresa of Avila says you can tell the life of prayer is going on because of the fruit growing in the garden. There are results of prayer life, natural things that happen. Fruit is a perfect illustration—it happens because of the life—it does not happen to make the life. I do not do good things so I can have this life, but because I have this life I can do good things. It is a natural evolution.

Newly committed Christians often speak of "leaving the world." God takes the focus away from the world and brings us into the banqueting house, where we are loved. This is the beginning of the journey. We might start attending church on a regular basis, or participating in more Christian activities. We need to be in the banqueting house because we need the love of the Body of Christ around us. We need the support in order to begin this journey. However, it is not long before we find the journey is not just from the world into the church; we find that the journey takes place inside as well, and "leaving the world" is going on within us.

This is not an external change. God draws us into the inner chamber, the inner dwellingplace. We find God's home is not the church building, but our hearts. This is the real banqueting house, the sanctuary is within ourselves. Our hearts are the temple of the Holy Spirit. This is the place God chooses for us to meet together, to listen and learn. In the beginning of our journey, it may be all right to learn from many different sources. We hear church teachers, listen to tapes, sing songs, read books, but the time comes when this learning does not suffice. We must go beyond and find God speaks to us individually, uniquely, deep within our very soul.

One of the problems with the spiritual journey is that many of us never know God speaks, and we never realize God speaks within us. We always think, "If I just get another book, another tape, another speaker, another teacher, a new person, somebody from that successful ministry . . . If I just listen to that person, then I am going to mature, then I am going to grow, then I will learn how to do it better. . . . I can always be better if I listen to some other great preacher." We want to use step one, two, and three. After awhile, we know by experience it does not work. The external message is not the indwelling of Christ. We must turn to the still, small voice dwelling within. It is not going to be a voice saying, ". . . Thus sayeth the Lord." That is too simple. The still, small voice is the silent invitation, the quiet infusion of knowledge, the wordless communication going on within—so silent and so deep we only know it when we meet with God.

It is inside God loves us, inside God transforms us. It is like adding leaven to bread—gradually changing the whole nature of the loaf. The same ingredients become something different. It is the same with us. The indwelling presence changes us somehow. We are still human. We are still flesh. We are still in this body, but because of the great transcendent God who comes to live in us, we change, little by little, transformed into Christ's image.

The goal of this journey is the image of Christ. It is union with God's will. If you read John 17:21 you'll see this repeated over and over, the message of union, of oneness.

Jesus says, "*. . . As you, Father, are in me and I am in you, may they also be in us, so that the world may believe that you have sent me.*"

God wants three different types of unity for us. One is unity with God, and this is the first part of our journey. Through God transforming us, we gain unity within ourselves. Finally, through God's continuing guidance, we discover unity with one another. The greatest commandment speaks about this, that we should love God above all things and love our neighbor as ourselves.

After we have entered the banqueting house, we learn to be at one with ourselves. Deep down inside we have a soul. The deepest center of our soul is where Christ dwells within us. It is this part of our being which is eternal. We are created in God's image. God does not say "you are a piece of junk until I put my Spirit in you." God says, "I created human beings in my image." In redemption, Jesus comes and indwells this image, living through us! Isn't this what scripture says? If we are created in the image of God, we must be pretty good. We have become sinful because of the Fall, but still good—still the image of God.

Isn't there a person deep within who you know is the real you, the person you would love to be, who maybe nobody else knows? Is there a person you have never had the courage to be? Hidden deep within is someone . . . someone you know is the real you.

God is saying, "Will the real you please stand up?!" The journey, besides getting to know and be in touch with God, is also finding union with ourselves.

We cannot get in touch with that inner person unless we get alone with God. Teresa of Avila says self-knowledge is almost as important as God-knowledge. Self-knowledge is twofold. First, we discover "I really am broken. I really am rejected." But the other revelation is: *"I can do all things through him who strengthens me."* (Philippians 4:13.)

God loves me, created me, chose me. We learn our inner person is a precious and beloved creature whom God has made—our inner person is the real creation of God.

Without the life of prayer, this idea will not make much sense. One can be a Christian all one's life, die and go to heaven, without ever fully realizing what God has done or intended. If we had just a glimpse of what it means to be in relationship with God, and the importance of that relationship, it would turn our whole world upside down. Instead of trying to fit in a little moment for prayer here and there, we would have an entire life of prayer, a life we would fit our "work" into. Prayer is where the changes happen. It is the relationship where God transforms us, and the healing takes place.

There are some realities in the journey. The first reality we begin to notice is the reality of God. We come to know the reality of our redemption. We come to know the indwelling Christ and the power of the Holy Spirit. This brings joy, blessing, and excitement. But you have to understand, it is an *unfolding* journey. It is continually unfolding and continually becoming. In the beginning of our journey, we may have a glimpse of the reality of God, but as we grow we will have a fuller and fuller revelation of that, a fuller and fuller revelation of what redemption really means.

The second reality God shows us is of our broken state, of our human nature, of our worldliness, of our attachments to things, and of our attitude. As God's light shines within us, we begin to see all the junk gathered in the corners of our lives—the junk we have never cleaned out—and it makes us penitent. It makes us remorseful. It makes us want to confess and get rid of the junk.

The third reality God brings us is *"I can do all things through him who strengthens me."* (Philippians 4:13.) In my weakness, God is strong. In Deuteronomy 7:6-9 it says,

> *"For you are a people holy to the Lord your God; the Lord your God has chosen you out of all the peoples on the earth to be his people, his treasured possession. It was not because you were more numerous than any other people that the Lord set his heart on you and chose you—for you were the fewest of all peoples. It was because the Lord loved you and kept the oath that he swore to your ancestors, that the Lord has brought you out with a mighty hand, and redeemed you from the house of slavery, from the hand of Pharaoh king of Egypt. Know therefore that the Lord your God is God; the faithful God who maintains covenant loyalty with those who love him and keep his commandments, to a thousand generations."*

These verses refer specifically to the Israelites, but they speak to us too. God is saying, "It was not because you were such a big deal. It was not because you were so important. I chose you because I love you." God *chose you*—in all your weakness. This is why God keeps a hand on you, why God keeps the covenant—not because you are great, but because God LOVES you. Isn't it simple?

God brings us out of unreality into the reality of love. Isaiah 43:4 says, *"Because you are precious in my sight, and honored, and I love you. . . ."* Isaiah 49:15 says,

> *"Can a woman forget her nursing child and show no compassion for the child of her womb? Even these may forget, yet I will not forget you."*

Imagine the kind of love a mother has for her nursing child . . . the verse goes on to say, *"See, I have inscribed you on the palms of my hands. . . ."* In Psalm 139:13-16 David praises God, saying:

> *"For it was you who formed my inward parts; you knit me together in my mother's womb. I praise you, for I am fearfully and wonderfully made. Wonderful are your works; that I know very well. My frame was not hidden from you, when I was being made in secret, intricately woven in the depths of the earth. Your eyes beheld my unformed substance. In your book were written all the days that were formed for me, when none of them as yet existed.*

Isaiah 43 says: *". . . I have redeemed you. I have called you by name, you are mine."* We are precious, honored, beloved, unforgotten—no longer rejected or scorned. We are loved. The lie is the rejection and the pain and the woundedness. The truth is: love and acceptance. We are *the chosen* of God our Creator.

God sees Jesus in us. God does not see the rejection, the scorn, the wounds and lies that we have believed about ourselves. We do not need to measure up to some standard to be acceptable. Out of love, God chose us! It takes a lifetime of hearing that, doesn't it? It takes a lifetime of God pressing love in, to set a person free.

Like Lazarus, raised and unbound, our role is simply to let it happen. Our role is to surrender. Our role is to be before God's presence, allowing the Holy Spirit's creative work to be done in us. We cannot make it happen ourselves. We cannot do the unbinding. In fact, we sin if we are continually fooling around, trying to make ourselves over, trying to be better, continually saying, "God cannot love me because I am like this; and God cannot love me because I am like that." If we have our vision focused on our own personhood, instead of beholding the glory of the Lord, we are sinning.

> *"And all of us, with unveiled faces, seeing the glory of the Lord as though reflected in a mirror, are being transformed into the same image from one degree of glory to another."* (II Corinthians 3:18.)

This is how we change. Not because we work it out ourselves, or we learn how to be better. We change as we melt in God's presence.

Looking at the following scripture verses, we can see the transformation. Exodus 34:29:

> *"As he came down from the mountain with two tablets of the covenant in his hands, Moses did not know that the skin of his face shone because he had been talking to God."*

Moses did not know it. The people said, "Moses, cover your face! We can't take it!" Moses didn't even know he was radiant. He had just been on the mountain talking with God.

Jesus would also withdraw to the wilderness to pray, going away to meet with the Father. And remember, John the Baptist says, *"The Father loves the Son . . ."* (John 3:35.) What a joyful reunion!

Think about Luke 6:12 and Luke 9:29:

"Now during those days he went out to the mountain to pray: and he spent the night in prayer to God."

"And while he was praying, the appearance of his face changed, and his clothes became dazzling white."

Now look at the blessing God gave Moses, who in turn gave it to Aaron, for the Israelites. Numbers 6:24-26:

"The Lord bless you and keep you; the Lord make his face shine upon you and be gracious to you; the Lord turn his face toward you and give you peace."

Moses spoke to God face to face, like a man speaks to his friend. Moses' face shone with the radiance of God because of the meeting. And now God says, "This is how you bless the people, say: *'The Lord make his face shine upon you.'*"

Psalm 24:3-7:
"Who shall ascend the hill of the Lord? And who shall stand in his holy place? Those who have clean hands and pure hearts, who do not lift up their souls to what is false, and do not swear deceitfully. They will receive blessing from the Lord, and vindication from the God of their salvation. Such is the company of those who seek him, who seek the face of the God of Jacob. Lift up your heads, O gates . . ."

Psalm 27:7-8:
"Hear, O Lord, when I cry aloud, be gracious to me and answer me! 'Come,' my heart says, 'seek his face!' Your face, O Lord, do I seek."

Psalm 31:16:
"Let your face shine upon your servant; save me in your steadfast love."

Psalm 67:1:
"May God be gracious to us and bless us and make his face to shine upon us."

Psalm 119:135:
"Make your face shine upon your servant and teach me in your decrees."

II Corinthians 3:7:
"But if the ministry of death, written and engraved on stones, was glorious, so that the children of Israel could not look steadily at the face of Moses because of the glory of his countenance, which glory is passing away, how will the ministry of the Spirit not be more glorious?"

II Corinthians 3:18:
"And all of us, with unveiled faces, seeing the glory of the Lord as though reflected in a mirror, are being transformed into the same image from one degree of glory to another; for this comes from the Lord, the Spirit."

The transformation does not come from us. It comes from God's Spirit. We are transformed by beholding God's glory. This is why it is so important to be with God, to take time, to allow God's face to shine upon us and change us. We are on a journey, a journey from one degree of glory to another, and we need to get our eyes off of ourselves and onto God. We have to be so released—so free—to keep our eyes on God, to behold God and let the Spirit have entrance into our lives.

We need to be like a child. Jesus says in Luke 18:16,

> *"Let the little children come to me, and do not stop them; for it is to such as these that the kingdom of God belongs."*

Remember the child running naked across the floor? And God said, *"Who told you that you were naked?"* Why are you embarrassed? Why are you self-conscious? Why are you afraid to state your opinion? Why are you afraid to say, "This is who I am?" Why are you afraid? Is it because you keep looking at yourself, examining yourself, instead of looking at God? Remember, Jesus is our mirror image. We can look at Jesus and reflect his image. Look at him. Look at him. Look at him and be radiant. Isn't this what scripture says?

<u>Scriptures for Meditation:</u>
Song of Solomon 2:13b-14,
Isaiah 48:17-19; 49:14-16,
John 17:26,
Psalm 16,
Deuteronomy 7:6,
II Corinthians 4:6-18; 5:16-21,
Colossians 3:1-4,
Psalm 145:1-3.

The following comes from *Spiritual Hilltops*, cRalph S. Cushman, Abingdon Press, 1960.

> *"Oh, let me grow!*
> *About me buds are bursting,*
> *And greening trees are yearning toward the sky,*
> *And everywhere is God's good power working*
> *The stagnant earth and lifting life on high*
>
> *Oh let me grow!*

Shall I alone be dying
When earth and sky obey his slightest nod?
Am I a dwarf in God's great universe defying
The Laws of life that lift men up to God?
Then let me grow!
This world is mere beginning;
Soul, thou are born for greater things than this;
Eternal mansions wait for greater things than this;
Eternal mansions wait thy ardent winning,
Adventures high, the battlements of God, thy
Master's kiss."

Amen.

Receiving God's Love

I have come full circle in my journey. I began by wanting to follow God, letting God take care of my every need. Then I ran my foot against a stone. I fell and landed on my face. It took me several years of recovery. I think God "broke all my bones" so I would heal correctly. This healing brought me back to the same place: "I see the Lord. I want to follow." There was nothing I could do about my weaknesses, nothing I could do about my personality faults. But I went through several years of thinking, "If I could just fix them I would be an acceptable person and then I would be accepted." I have come full circle to believing there is absolutely nothing I can do about my condition. Only God can transform me. My role is to seek God's face. This is why the old writers say spiritual life grows more simple—because the more we get to know God, the more we realize we cannot, by our own reason or strength, do anything. We cannot!

We are to seek God's face. Our role is to allow God's face to shine on us and bless us—not to look at ourselves, not to look at what is not yet finished, or at the mistakes that will come. All we can do is confess what we know to be sin, and forget it. Do we have to keep punishing ourselves because of our sin forever and ever? Do we have to keep going back over everything we have done in our lives, feeling guilty? If we do, then we make Jesus' cross nothing—that *he died for nothing*. We have to receive forgiveness. We have to accept the washing of the blood of Jesus. We have to do this in order to say, "What you did had effect. What you did worked in my life."

We need to seek God's face and come into God's presence with the complete abandon a child would have: totally unaware of our nakedness, focused outward, focused on God instead of on self. We need to come unashamedly into God's presence. How can we do this? How can we get to the place where we can come in? One way is by meditating on scripture, particularly on the parts of scripture which say things like, *"Because you are precious in my sight . . ."*

Let the words soak in: God says this with many different words,

> *"I have redeemed you; I have called you by name, you are mine. When you pass through the waters, I will be with you; and through the rivers, they shall not overwhelm you; when you walk through the fire you shall not be burned, and the flame shall not consume you."* (Isaiah 41:1-2.)

Pray verses like these, meditate on them, let the words soak in to replace all the lies laid up inside you over the years.

Focusing the other way, thinking, "Oh, how can this be true for me? Maybe it is true for everybody else, but not for me," is self-centeredness. Sometimes we have the idea self-centeredness is saying, "I am really good and I am really big and important." Maybe it is. Anything centering on "I" all the time probably is self-centered. But self-centeredness is also this: "Well, poor me, I am so unworthy, I am so bad, I am so rejected." This is self-centeredness, too. "Nobody pays any attention to me, nobody likes me, I am not acceptable." This is centering on self. Sometimes we think of this as humility, but humility is being yourself and fully human. Fully Christ-like is fully humble and human.

We meditated on Deuteronomy 7:6 earlier, *"The Lord your God has chosen you out of all the peoples on earth to be his people, his treasured possession."* We need to create space in our lives so we have the opportunity to receive this sunshine, to receive God's face. *Sonshine.* We must have time to get in front of God, see God's face and receive the blessing. We need to allow time to be alone with the God who loves us so much! We must take time to let God love us. This is the most healing thing we can do: to be in a place of prayer and receive God's love.

You may not *realize* God's love at first. But the more you are present to God, the more you turn to God, the more you will begin to experience Love. God's presence *is* love. When you dwell in the love, there is healing. Have you ever experienced God's presence within? It does not require words, it does not require any knowledge on our part. It is a secret transfusion that goes on, and one changes because of it. You do not have to have an explicit situation. It does not have to be, "This happened to me and therefore I am healed of a certain thing;" or, "I went through this circumstance and now I am healed of this;" or "God showed me this and I worked it out and now I have learned something new." It is a secret and hidden wisdom infused in us by the very presence of God, requiring no words, no transmission of thought. It just happens. It is as if God presses in on you and you change because of God's presence. Being loved changes us. Being loved by God changes us. Our prayers, "God change me, God heal me, God take this away, God change my personality, God do this for me, do that for me" will not change us like simply being with God and receiving love.

Intercession, praying for others, is such a wonderful thing to do! But it does not usually change us. In fact, it is a real good way to "hop over" and avoid the issues of our own lives. We need to allow God's presence to shine into the deep places. We can share our needs with God if we want. We can share anything we want. We do not have to just sit there. If you feel like talking to God, that is fine, but simply being present is fine too, and *it will change you.*

Set aside specific time to be with God, like Jesus did. Go into the *wilderness,* on the mountain, or in the *desert.* Go into solitude with God. Teresa of Avila was known to stay up until one or two o'clock in the morning to write, so she could spend the prime hours of her day in God's presence. Remember Psalm 16:11 which says: *". . . In your presence there is fullness of joy."* There is real joyful friendship in God's presence. We need to spend our *best* times with God.

The following quote comes from a book called The Quiet Way, translated by Emily Chisholm. It includes selected writings from Gerhard Tersteegen, a Protestant theologian who lived in the seventeenth century and wrote during the Thirty Years War. He speaks of prayer:

> "Pray if you like, but not without worship.
>
> . . . You say you cannot pray? Is there then no oh, no ah in your heart? And granted you cannot find even that, when you say you cannot pray, you are praying.
>
> . . . Let deep call unto deep and let this be your prayer when you cannot make any other. . . . Prayer is looking at God who is ever present and letting Him look at us."

Prayer is more than just saying things to God. God is not limited by our words or by what we understand. Do we fool God by our words? Have you ever heard it said, "Do not say 'Thy will be done' because then God will think you do not have enough faith."? This seems to imply God does not know how you really feel. How can God *not know* what we think and feel, or if we ache inside? Every groan is a prayer, every desire, every longing. These can *be* prayer.

We have such a limited understanding of what prayer is and what intercession is. The very words, the thought, "I cannot pray," the longing for God, the groan of our heart, this is prayer!

Tersteegen says more wonderful things:

> "You must withdraw into yourself a little and keep quiet before the face of God. Then look gently and perfectly frankly, at God, who is so near to us, to let Him see if there is anything in us or near us which must be handed over, and assure Him of our hardy consent to give up everything to Him. Remain exposed to Him in the light of truth simply, in this way, without any investigations or scruples of your own for as long as God gives grace. Since then I am neither willing nor able to row against the wind, I let my little ship go into it. If only I take care not to stick fast on some sand bank of selfishness, let come what may, even if I suffer shipwreck, it will only be in the ocean of God whose depths are as good as the best harbor."

Sometimes spiritual life is like a leaf flowing in the stream. You can let it go. It will go where it is supposed to go. Just be in the stream: setting aside time, being there, opening up to God, letting

God have you. From a practical standpoint, the greatest prayer is: "I love you." Saying those words to God, over and over again, will transform your life: "I love you, God. I love you. I love you." Couple that kind of prayer time with learning to abide in God's presence. Learn to turn to God all day long. Learn to fellowship with God in your heart all day long. Learn to recall God's presence all day long. No two practices will better insure spiritual growth than these. It is a very simple life. Turn to God. Jesus said in John 8:29: *"And the one who sent me is with me; he has not left me alone."* Be with God. Speak lovingly to God in your heart all day long: "You are precious. I love you, God. I love you, Jesus. Thank you, Jesus. Bless you, Jesus." Worship God all day long. Think about being created to walk in the garden with God, whose very nature is love. Remember Genesis 1:27: *"So God created humankind in his image, in the image of God he created them."* We are partakers of the "divine nature."

We are created to love. Our real nature is love, and the perfect image of God is love. As we love and worship God, speak our love, we move along the stream of life. Moment by moment, we "see" God, every moment we are present, sharing love with God. Unreality is un-love, rejection, brokenness, bitterness, hurt, centeredness on self. Reality is union, oneness, compassion, selflessness, unconditional self-giving love.

Reality is learning to see God in the very stuff of everyday existence, moment by moment. It is not just during worship with church groups. Some folks think enjoying the spiritual life means attending church groups or being with church friends, listening to Christian tapes, reading Christian books, or going to Christian events. Yet God *is in every moment*. When we start coming together with God and experiencing oneness, we begin to see that God is everywhere. God's creative power is in everything. God gives life to every blade of grass. God is not every blade of grass—that is pantheism. But God is in every blade of grass. God is in nature and speaks to us in nature. Why do we like to walk in the woods and smell the flowers? We are drawn closer to God. We see our Creator through flowers and grass, sunsets and oceans, dirt and trees, stars and landscapes, birds and trees.

God meets us through everything, not just through the beauty of nature. My aunt from the farm used to say, "I don't know how anyone could live in the city, it's so ugly!" But, I think it is so beautiful! I love the city! I can walk down the street and breathe God's presence. Why is that? Could it be because God is with me? If you are there, God is there, *everywhere*. God blesses the ordinary. God blesses human life. God blesses the everyday stuff of life. When our eyes are open and unveiled, we see God everywhere.

Think of God: omnipotent, all-powerful, magnificent, creator of the universe, very God of very God, begotten, not made. This great, omniscient, infinite God became a baby. God just went poof! and popped out in nature—a baby! God could have come as the Taj Mahal, or St. Peter's Cathedral, or any of the great seven wonders of the world, even Kilamanjaro. But God did not. God breathed forth this magnificent creative power and created a little teeny baby. Isn't it incredible? It is so amazing! We say, "God, show yourself to us," and we see Jesus in a stable, a carpenter's shop, a little town; and he sometimes had no place to lay his head. We see him poor, walking in a country drier than bone, walking in the sand with dust on his feet. Imagine, he must have been covered in dust all the time! All of this because we said, "God, manifest yourself to us, show us your beauty, your nature." This is what we received. Of all the things God could have done, we received this baby, this child, this man. God incarnate.

What a profound, amazing, incredible way to say to us, "I'm here in the very stuff of life, in the very ordinary things, in everything that you confront, moment by moment, every day. Open your eyes and see me."

How many people went past the stable and only smelled the barn? How many? Out of all those people who were in Bethlehem for the census, how many could have come? How many could have gathered around that place? But the people in Bethlehem did not notice. It was probably no big deal to be born in a stable. In fact, Mary and Joseph were probably fortunate she was not in the street having her baby on a blanket donated by Lutheran World Relief!

Jesus' friends—who were they? Were they the scribes, the Pharisees, the Roman leaders? No. Among them there was a prostitute, a tax collector, a leper, a revolutionary, and some fishermen. He could have chosen anybody. He could have made a wonderful life for himself. But God manifested in Jesus—in the everyday, in the ordinary. Today it is the very same thing. We need to be present in the ordinary, all day long, to God. We do not see it when our vision is clouded over with the negative, the selfish, the self-centered, the junk. We do not see. But if we would live moment by moment, with God, we would see.

Frank Laubach, in <u>Practicing His Presence</u>, wrote about this same thing. Laubach said all of his years in ministry were nothing compared to what happened to him after he started practicing the presence of God, turning his thoughts to God all day long. He said God transformed his thoughts to God all day long. He said God transformed his little hut there in the Philippines into a tabernacle filled with God's glory. He said it seemed like all the rest of his life was wasted. And the same can be true for us when we start receiving God, opening up to God, in every moment of our life, moment by moment: "I love you, I love you, I love you." Pretty soon we will see things that we did not see before.

When we get our eyes off of ourselves and on God, every day, every event, every situation becomes an icon, a window, to God. We can learn to reflect upon these things. We will see and hear what God is speaking to us. No more: "God isn't saying anything to me. . . . God never says anything, I am so dry, I do not hear anything. . . . I am trying to get wisdom. . . . I am trying to make decisions. . . . I need to make decisions. . . . I need to know, God is not speaking. . . . Why don't I hear?" We do not hear because we are not present to God, we are listening for the wrong thing. But when we open up and are present to God in every moment, we begin to hear God's voice.

I have my own vision of how God speaks. It is like looking out at the Pacific, at this immense ocean, with a huge wave coming at me. I am standing there ready to be engulfed in this huge wave and God says, "This is me speaking all the time." All I have to do is learn how to hear it, all day long, every moment of existence. God is always speaking, always pouring out. God is always there. We just need to learn how to open up and listen. We just need to learn how to hear.

Tilden Edwards, in Living Simply Through the Day, says:

> "Prayer is opening to love, into that radiant and centeredness love, surpassing our understanding and enfolding all of life. The truly holy person is wholly open in

> this living presence through every happening of the day. This is the root of that person's simplicity and consistency and capacity to see through everything to this shared core that shines through all. The highest saint's life is one continuous prayer, one seamless participation in holy reality through all its forms."
>
> And he says, "Special prayer time simply is an opportunity to give special attention to this opening."

In other words, "set aside" prayer time is not different, it is simply a time in which you can give special attention. It is like working together with your spouse all day long, and then taking a special time to just be alone with each other. This "set aside" prayer time is simply an opportunity to give special attention to this opening to love. So many of our daily experiences can cloud, warp and close this natural openness. Without special time to cultivate love, we easily sink deeper into confusion and craziness. But with careful, conscious attention, it seeps into the happenings of the day. Instead of becoming more fragmented and defensive, we see the underlying unity. We slowly become more capable of discriminating the incredibly dense and deceptive cloudiness in and around us from the always present sun hidden beneath.

As we walk in the fullness of God's presence, we can experience that presence with us all day long, and the events of our lives take on different meanings. God speaks to us, and gives meaning through the things we experience every day. We begin to see God's creative movement within us through events. God is able to transform us into the image of Jesus, healing and revealing truth in our inward parts, gathering our fragmented self into union with God.

Scriptures for Meditation:
Psalm 3:3-6; 17:15; 18:1,
Isaiah 55:1-3; 6-9,
Ephesians 5:15-20,
Philippians 4:4-9,
Colossians 1:15-27.

Lord, grant us revelation in the inward parts. Grant us truth. Show us how to lift our eyes off of ourselves and onto your glorious face, to receive your own abounding grace, to have life and have it abundantly. We pray this in Jesus' name.

Learning to Love

The little things that bug me, resentments deep within
The things I ought to do, undone,
The irritations one by one;
Till nerves stretch, screaming thin and bare
For all the world to see.
Which needs his touch to make it whole the most:
My body or my soul?
I pray but nothing comes out right.
My thoughts go flying everywhere,
My attitudes are all confused;
I hate myself, I am not used.
Two hands all clenched, not clasped in prayer;
And heart too leaden to take flight.
Which, oh which, needs to be whole the most:
My body or my soul?

I cannot read, I cannot pray, I cannot even think.
Where to from here, and how to get there
With only darkness everywhere?
I ought to rise and only sink;
And feel his arms and hear him say,
"I love you."
It was all my soul and my body needed to be whole.

by Ruth Bell Graham

Thank you, Lord, for accepting us just where we are, for clasping us in your arms and saying, "I love you." It's all we need to make us whole. Amen.

This poem speaks of reality. Sometimes we want to separate the soul from the body. We can be spiritual, but falling apart emotionally and physically. God loves the whole person. God loves the tense body and the muscle spasms in the back, the clenched teeth, and all those natural things about us. We are human and life sometimes is not easy to live.

We are on a journey, a journey into reality. That reality is union. Oneness. It is oneness with God, ourselves, and with others. When we forget about ourselves and our own weaknesses and frailties, and just abandon ourselves to God—when we just let go and let God have us—then God begins to take down the walls of hostility inside of us.

When God loves us inside, we can afford to let the walls down, because God's love changes the way we feel about ourselves. God can remove all the barriers we use to protect ourselves. As the barriers go down, we experience more complete union with God. We are able to experience, in a very real way, God's presence within us *every moment* of the day.

When God takes down the walls of self-protection, we find the walls that separate us from one another also fall down. Sometimes our own walls might come down, but the walls of our neighbor might still be rigidly in place. You might question whether or not we can have oneness if our walls are down and someone else's are still up. How can we have oneness, how can we have unity in this case? We do not have to figure it out! All we need to worry about is the unity God wants to work in us. When God takes down our walls, we will find love flowing out unconditionally. Isn't this the way God loves? God does not wait until our walls are down, or we are ready. God does not wait until we can receive and then love back. God just loves us.

As we experience God's unconditional love for ourselves, we become unafraid to be vulnerable. God makes us open, so love can flow out to others, even when they do not love us back. Much of our fear of loving is because we are afraid we are not going to be loved back. But what if we say, "It makes no difference if I am loved back?" What does it hurt if I just love and am not loved back? Does it make any difference?

Personally, God has taught me much about unconditional love. I used to be afraid to love. I did not like being so vulnerable. But God kept saying, "You must not do that, you must love." And I would say, "Okay, God! All right! If that is what you want, I will love even if it hurts. I will love even if . . ." Then as soon as I felt too vulnerable, I would immediately clutch my love up again and hold onto myself and protect myself. I would have to go through all the work with God *again*. God would work in me over and over again until I would get to the place where I could say, "Okay, I will love with no conditions." I finally realized God was going to keep working in me, and it was time to love that way, *no matter what happened.*

What does this mean? What does it mean to love freely, without any conditions? It means to love those who pound the nails in your hand, to love those who reject you, who spit on you, who make fun of you, who want to push you over a cliff. Those are the ones you love unconditionally.

What does unconditionally mean? It means that you love with no strings attached. We are just *to love*. It is the strangest thing, isn't it? Just to love, even if we get nothing in return. Just to love! We are transformed inside. We let love be, even if it is not received, even if it is rejected. Oh, to have the wonderful feeling inside that it does not matter! It takes years of responding to God for this to happen. It is not an overnight thing. We will not always win in the situation either. But we have to allow God to do the healing in us, so we can know it is no longer necessary for others to love us in order that we might have self-worth.

God cares for me. God loves me. I am precious. I am chosen, created by God, loved even if I make mistakes. God loves me even when I have said the wrong thing, when I have done the wrong thing, even when I have blown the whole works. Remember Psalm 139: *"In your book were written all the days that were formed for me, when none of them as yet existed."*

It is a blessing to me, to know God chooses me, redeems me, fills me with the Spirit, lives in me and uses me—even though God knows I will blow it over and over again. God knows my mistakes before I even make them, and still loves me, still cares, still chooses me. Even though God knew what a screw-up I would be at times, knew the numbers of times I would say, "I do not want to do this,"—I was still chosen! This was a very important revelation for me—that God knows everything and still loves me.

So I can set down all my weapons. God loves me. When we can see this—that we can be vulnerable and be endlessly received, we can make mistakes and be always forgiven—then it is not so hard to love unconditionally. My self-worth is not dependent on somebody else loving me, or somebody else thinking I am right, or somebody else accepting me, or somebody else saying "Well done thou good and faithful servant." None of those things really make any difference, because my self-worth comes from God. Therefore, we are free to love unconditionally.

Even if somebody else's walls are up, you can have your own walls down. This is Christ's love: selfless, self-giving, self-denying. *This is the very nature of God-in-us, love-in-us, loving the world.* We no longer look at one another from a human point of view. We see this in II Corinthians 5:16-17:

> *"From now on, therefore, we regard no one from a human point of view; even though we once knew Christ from a human point of view, we know him no longer in that way. So if anyone is in Christ, there is a new creation: everything old has passed away; see, everything has become new!"*

> *"Beloved, we are God's children now; what we will be has not yet been revealed. What we do know is this: when he is revealed, we will be like him for we will see him as he is."*

We can accept others because we realize that we are all *becoming*. Acceptance of others depends on the union of love we have with God. When we can accept others where they are at, as unique and special and gifted, then we do not have to be afraid of contamination from those who are different from us. This is part of the journey to reality. We come to a place in our spiritual walk where we are not afraid of everybody who looks or acts a little different than us.

The Body of Christ consists of those in union with Christ, those with the Spirit of Christ within them. This is the Body of Christ. Maybe it does not look the same in everyone, but it is still the Body of Christ. We can associate with Christians who are different from ourselves, people who are being called forth in unique, creative, different ways, without fear. Fear is a real quencher of renewal, fear of contamination by association: "Do not go here, do not talk to these people, do not read this book, do not listen to this music, do not do this, do not do that." Psalm 121:7-8 says:

"The Lord will keep you from all evil; he will keep your life; the Lord will keep your going out and your coming in from this time on and forevermore."

Now, if you are a blatant sinner out there doing whatever you want, you cannot expect to walk under God's protection. But when you are seeking God with all your heart and led by the Spirit, you do not have to fear! No more thinking: ". . . If I talk to the wrong people, I might get something, something might leech onto me."

We, who are created in the image of Christ, need only to love our neighbors unconditionally. We, who see through the glass darkly, do not have the whole picture of what it means to know the Lord; and our neighbor on the journey also sees through a glass darkly and does not have the whole picture. Maybe we have just as many blatant heresies as the other person does. We simply cannot see our own heresies. We can only see the other person's, and we are afraid to death of them. Exposure to his or her heresies might make me like him or her. Isn't this the way we sometimes think?

Reality is when you are being transformed into the image of Christ, when you are like Christ. God calls *you* forth and you do not need to worry about anyone else. You will be created as God intends, your neighbor will be created as God intends, and there is nothing you can do about it except to love unconditionally.

Jesus was not picky. He could have had Caiaphas for his friend. He could have had the entire Sanhedrin, the Scribes, and the Pharisees. He could even have had some Roman soldiers, people with authority. But whom did he choose? He befriended a prostitute, a tax collector, a leper, even a woman who was the wife of one of Herod's people.

Jesus was not afraid of being contaminated. He loved his friends unconditionally. This is reality, the reality God wants for the Church. God wants the Church to be Christ-like and loving. The Church is wherever inner union is taking place, and we are one with every single person who has Christ growing within, regardless of their outward denomination or their doctrines. Wherever Christ is, so too is the Church, and we are one with the Church. When we know it is the life of Christ within us transforming us, it is not a certain set of principles, laws or doctrines, then we can love the Church wherever we find it.

When we set up doctrines and rules and principles, instead of loving unconditionally, when we say, "This is how we all have to live now," we deny the freedom of Christ's love. Galatians 5:1 says: *"For freedom Christ has set us free. Stand firm, therefore, and do not submit again to the yoke of slavery."*

Throughout much of my own journey, God has worked in me, in the area of fear: fear of relationships, fear of different groups, fear of deception, etc. My worst fear was that of being deceived. I finally had to get to the place in my journey where I believed in God's sovereignty, and that God knew all I'd need to go through; that God is the author and finisher of my faith, and is big enough to see me through even deception. It was the only way I could be free to continue on in my journey.

A few years ago, I had to go to Washington for two weeks of residency. God did all these wonderful things to get me there. I was accepted into the program regardless of late registration and waiting lists. I received the money I needed. All these wonderful things occurred in my outward circumstances to get me to Washington. There were twenty-six other people from different denominations in the program, and I was the only person from my denomination. We all started praying, and I thought, "How did I get here? I do not think I want to be in this place." They prayed differently than I prayed and there were some things with which I did not agree. I thought, "Can I be here? Maybe I need to get out of here. When does the next plane leave?"

God said to me that night, "I did a lot of things to get you here, now stay and learn!" My experience there became a high point in my spiritual life—one of the most renewing experiences of my life. Never have I been so affirmed as a person, so aware of what God has done in me. I experienced such freedom to be myself and I experienced such community with all those people from many different walks of life. God showed me something about the Body of Christ and about fear. Just when we think we have our doctrine all sewed up, we realize we only see a little glimpse of God's plan. We are like the blind trying to describe an elephant.

We make mistakes, all of us do, and we need to allow the next person to make his or her own mistakes. It does not mean we have to adhere to, or even accept their beliefs, but instead that we do not need to fear or hate or judge them. *We do have to love unconditionally.* Real Christianity goes beyond doctrine and beyond narrow Pharisee-ism, it is *to love.* The greatest sign of the presence of Christ is love, not gifts. John 13:35 says, *"By this everyone will know that you are my disciples, if you have love for one another."*

I Corinthians 12:4-6 says:

> *"Now there are varieties of gifts, but the same Spirit; and there are varieties of services, but the same Lord; and there are varieties of activities, but it*

is the same God who activates all of them in everyone."

Who has the truth? Jesus. We are one body with many members in each congregation, each denomination, one body with many members in the whole Church. Some are evangelical members, some are peace and justice members, some are prophetic members, and we are all parts of the same Body. We all need each other.

I John 3:14 says, *"We know that we have passed from death to life because we love one another. Whoever does not love abides in death."*

Atonement. At-one-ment. Oneness, unity, this is reality. It is something that happens to us as we are being transformed from one degree of glory to another.

Let it happen! Love unconditionally! Do not worry about "What is happening to me? Am I losing it? Am I forgetting that I am a Christian? Are my morals changing?" No, you are becoming one with Christ, and Jesus loves unconditionally. Love people where they are. Love them into the Kingdom like Jesus did. He did not hit people over the head with the truth. He sat and ate with them. He loved them. Perfect love casts out fear. I John 4:12, *"No one has ever seen God; if we love one another, God lives in us, and his love is perfected in us."*

<u>Scriptures for Meditation</u>:
Galatians 2:19-21,
Galatians 5:1-6,
Colossians 2:16-3:4,
I John 3:14,
I John 4:7-21.

Gerhard Tersteegen writes:

> "When he (another churchman) knows what I think of separation, church government, or as he calls it, sectarianism, or whether he doesn't can help neither his soul nor mine. And whether our opinions on that subject are similar or different does not make us one hair's breadth holier or more blessed. When I have the chance of hearing a godly Reformed or Lutheran preacher, I go to church, and if I had a chance of getting to know a godly Catholic preacher, I would listen to his sermon in the very same freedom of spirit, although I might not always avail myself of this freedom because of the weakness of others. Wherever there's a man who fears God and lives a good life, in any country under the sun, God is there loving him, and so I love him too, whatever religious coat he may be wearing. And so it is quite true, I do go about with people of all sorts of religious persuasions. I talk to them publicly or privately as God disposes about denying God, about prayer, and about loving God, and I let the whole edifice of their particular church government and doctrine stand quite untouched as long as God lets it stand.
>
> "Love alone is not walled in by divisions. Love is universal, it flows out into the infinite, for it proceeds from the Father and the Son and takes into its wide embrace all who will let themselves be gathered in. And it is my hope that soon all the scattered children of God will creep in once more to this, the true fold of the church, and without any of the labors,

forms and contrivances of men become one blessed flock with one shepherd. For love will win in the end, but it will be that pure love of God which is poured out in true fellowship with the Father and the Son in the hearts of those who strive to walk in the light, turning from the shadow to the substance, from the outer to the inner and from all multiplicity to the one thing needful. This alone brings us union with one another and peace with God."

Amen.

Loving Unconditionally

We are being transformed into the image of God, into Christ-likeness, by virtue of the indwelling Christ. This transformation is not because of our good works, not because we are doing all these wonderful things, but because we have a great treasure in this earthen vessel. Daily, our "self-life" is being put to death so the life of Christ might be made manifest through the earthen vessel. There is light shining out of darkness. As we meet God in the tabernacle of our hearts, as God shines the light of a loving countenance upon us, we are transformed from one degree of glory to another. As we grow in this love union, God heals our inner person, God brings truth to our inward parts, and God calls forth the uniqueness of our creation. As we learn to live and love in God's presence, unconditional love takes down the walls of separation and hostility within us. God takes away our fears and we are able to receive love and love in return.

Because God loves us, we can love unconditionally. We can accept others in their unique *createdness*, where they are instead of where we think they should be. When we ourselves are loved unconditionally, we allow others the freedom to become Christ-like. We set our defenses down. Then others can remove their defenses. They are no longer afraid of being rejected because of who they are or because of how they feel about something.

One of the things which comes from unconditional love is "adult-adult" conversation. We do not have to skirt around an issue when we talk. We do not have to explain our actions and give all kinds of details. When we learn we are loved unconditionally, we can quit fearing rejection because we have said or done the "wrong" thing. I will still love you—no matter what you say. This may seem simple to you, but it is not simple.

We learn to speak with each other without fear that we will lose our friendship. We no longer have to wonder "What did you mean by that?" because we have given each other the freedom to become Christ-like. I am not perfect, and I sometimes do and say things that are very hurtful. We all do. But in unconditional love, we give each other the freedom to grow, to change—to *become*. When we experience God's love and are healed, we are freed to be ourselves; and then we are able to set others free. We can love them with the same unconditional love of Christ, not caring whether we are accepted or loved back: "I love you, just the way you are. And you are set free."

We become like an ingrown toenail if we limit our fellowship to those who are the "same". The language others speak, the terminology they use does not matter. If we cloister ourselves up we miss the richness of the variety of the Body of Christ. We love all who are joined to Christ, all who are on this inward journey, being transformed from one degree of glory to another. We love all who share the inward love with God, despite their doctrines and outward practices.

In the last chapter I wrote of my experience with the different people in my residency in Washington. The heritage of all their different traditions was so rich—we miss something when we do not learn about other traditions. Do you know it was John Calvin, forefather of the Methodist Church, who said, "My heart I give Thee, Lord, willingly and forever."? His symbol is a picture of a heart and a hand. "My heart I give

Thee, willingly and forever." Heart in a hand—it is so beautiful.

We miss something if we do not listen to the well of living water coming from other traditions. If we think narrowly, we miss the living water, and this is exactly how we get into all kinds of strange ideas and all kinds of strange practices. When we get into our own well too deep, pretty soon we lose sight of the original idea—loving God.

One group of people I meet with is predominantly Lutheran pastors. I see their hunger and thirst for God, and their desire for their congregations to grow spiritually. We come together to look for ways to introduce their congregations to a deep and intimate life with God. When we shut ourselves off from the rest of the Body of Christ, we miss these deeply committed people.

By coming into relationship with people from all different aspects of the Church, and not placing expectations on them, to listen to them without judging them, we can grow. This is how we want people to accept us, not placing expectations on us, not asking us to be something we are not, not asking us to perform in a way we cannot or do not know. We can only be who we are, and this is all we can expect of someone else.

We are created to love all who are joined to Christ's Body, no matter how they express their faith. As we are being recreated into Christ's image, the image of God, we can hear Jesus say, ". . . As the Father has sent me, I am sending you." (John 20:21) Christ sends us out. We are taken out of this world, into God's banqueting house. Then we are sent out again. In II Corinthians 5:18, Paul says some very interesting things:

> *"All this is from God, who reconciled us to himself through Christ, and has given us*

the ministry of reconciliation; that is, in Christ God was reconciling the world to himself, not counting their trespasses against them, and entrusting the message of reconciliation to us."

Paul does not say God waited until people quit sinning before reconciling them, but instead God was in Christ reconciling the world. God was not counting sins, but entrusting to us the message of reconciliation. We are to be ambassadors of Christ, allowing God to make the appeal through us for reconciliation. The Christ in us offers the hope of glory. God takes us out of the world and brings us into the banqueting house so we can be healed, transformed and then sent out again.

God will not send you out until you are ready. Do not ever get into, "Well, I should be . . .," or "I ought to . . ." When it is time for you to go out, you will know it because you will feel the desire to go out, you will have the urge to go out. Do not try to make it happen, but let it happen to you. Jesus lived in Nazareth for thirty years before he went out. Paul went into Arabia for a long time before he began traveling. Teresa of Avila was forty years old before she started doing anything significant, and she had been cloistered for twenty-some of those years. There is a time to be in God's inner chamber, and there is a time to be sent out.

When God sends you out, it might not be to an organized mission or ministry. It might just be to your neighbor. It might just be to the person down the street. My neighborhood has one house where the thirty-seven year old mother had a cerebral hemorrhage and died in the arms of her children. That is on one corner of the block. Across the street, the guy walked out, after twenty-some years of marriage, leaving three sons and his wife for some other person. Our next door neighbor's mother is dying of Alzheimer's and tried to set their house on fire, and accused them of stealing all her money. On the next corner there is one family with a child in prison.

Unless I can be with these people, the people closest to my home, how can I go anywhere else and be the Body of Christ for anyone else? When God sends us out, it is not always to some ministry; it might be to the neighbors. It might be to the people at your workplace. Be the Body of Christ for them. Be what they need. It might be to the poor, to the lonely. God sends us to a place where we can love unconditionally as Jesus has loved us. God sends us to our neighbors.

We are transformed into the image of Christ so we can be Christ in the midst of the world—loving the poor, loving the lonely, loving the lost—not necessarily to talk about Christ, but to *be* Christ to someone.

I know a young Christian woman who has made friends on the street. She has made real friends, not only "potentials" for the Kingdom, but friends. She is not looking for every opportunity to get a word in, to slip a tract, to leave a book. Instead, she listens to her friends. One of these friends was abused by her father. One is on drugs. Another person is a boy who is trying to stay straight after treatment, who knows he can call her and talk to her and she will help him stay clean. Another friend had scabies and got pregnant. This young Christian woman became her labor coach and held her hand while having a C-section. She has even stayed overnight to take care of the baby so her friend could get a night's rest. I think these people have seen Jesus . . . in a black leather jacket.

We are called to be Christ in the midst of the world. All of these young people have seen *Jesus* and all of them know it is God's love with which they are being loved. It takes years. Sometimes, to walk with someone and be a friend takes years. One of my professors tells of a woman he has been meeting with for thirty years. Thirty years! She has never accepted Christ, but she knows he loves Christ. Now she is asking him about the Jesus he loves. He said it has been worth it. He said, "We have had a wonderful relationship." But how many of us would have walked with her for thirty years?

My professor is Christ to this woman in the way Christ was to us. Jesus did not demand our love, did he? He did not demand it. He loved us until we came. When Christ takes possession of us and inhabits this temple, he wants to live his love through us. And he sends us out.

Sometimes I wonder how open our churches are to the lost. How many of us could invite in the lepers and the prostitutes and the chemically dependent? Or do we set them all on the back burner because they do not measure up? How many black leather jackets do we want in the front pews in our church; how many people would we want with red, green and blue-spiked hair? Some of these people know how to love better than we do. They really do.

Can we love those who have made mistakes—those who have fallen, who are struggling to get back? Can we love those who have been hurt by institutionalized religion and never want to set foot in another church? Can we love these people until they meet Jesus and find out he is not the institutionalized church, but he is a real and living person who lives within us and transforms us into his image, into his glory?

Scriptures for Meditation:
John 3:16-17,
Matthew 25:31-46,
James 2:1-17,
I Corinthians 2:6-10,
II Corinthians 1:3-7,
I John 3:16-18.

Lord Jesus, we thank you for the ways you have spoken to our hearts. You have let the light of your countenance shine upon us. Continue, Lord, to reveal to our hearts the truth, the truth that sets us free: that we are chosen, beloved and precious, and you have created us for yourself, you long to manifest your glory in us and through us, you long to reconcile the lost and the lonely and the broken to yourself through us. Jesus, make us vessels of love, let your love shine out of these earthen vessels. We want to be all that you created us to be. Lord, speak to our hearts. We pray in your name, Jesus. Amen.

Discovering Wholeness

Whenever we talk about the need for the journey, or the things which will happen in the journey, I am always afraid people are going to start thinking, "Oh, now I have to start doing this, and now I need to start doing that." We do not have to start. We *already* think this way and we *already* do some of these things. It is okay to do what you are doing. It is all right to feel the way you feel. As changes begin to happen in us, we need to avoid thinking as if something is "wrong" with us.

Particularly with the change from active prayer to contemplative prayer, it is easy to think "... Something is wrong with me . . . I should be praying more . . . I should be claiming and naming and standing and doing." But all we really want to do is sit at God's feet and love. Our adversary is saying to us, "Well, you are not even praying, you know, how can you call yourself a pray-er if you do not even pray? You think you are a big intercessor. You do not even know how to pray." We hear this kind of thing within ourselves. In fact, people who pray probably experience this kind of "attack" more. We experience feelings of accusation, we worry about backsliding, we question our Christianity. But God is faithful in keeping the covenant and shows mercy to those doing the seeking. We can believe in God's faithfulness and disbelieve all the accusations coming into our minds.

When we really try to seek God, to give ourselves to God, we feel these accusations because we have always experienced fragmentation between that which is sacred and that which is secular. We have experienced a separation between the sacred and the secular.

God is very smart; meeting us where we are, on our sense level. God meets us the way we have always experienced things—through what we see, feel, taste, touch, and so on. God takes us out of the world and into the banqueting house, takes us away from those things which are not good for our spiritual growth.

We find the things leading us away from God very distasteful; there is a real separation in our minds about what is spiritual or sacred and what is secular. This is a very natural part of God's call in our lives. But the time comes when the fragmentation is gone. God takes us and heals us and puts us together, and then we do not feel the same distaste, or accusation, or fragmentation. We are sent out to love, *unconditionally*.

It is all right to acknowledge that we do change, we do grow, and we are not always going to look at things in the same way. However, there is a lot of Christianity "boxed-in" this way. You know how it is: this is how you act if you are not a Christian and this is how you act if you are. This is where you go if you are not a Christian and this is where you should go. We cloister up in these little groups and do things "the right way." We have our patterns and our structures and our doctrines.

Here you come seeking, this pray-er, this contemplative, this person panting for God. You are saying, "Do it to me God, take me, change me, kill me, put me to death, do whatever you have to do, but make me like Christ." All of a sudden you find you are all alone in the seeking. You are bored to death in your little cloister doing your little routine. You wonder, "Don't you see there's a whole world out there?" You think, "What is happening to me? Is something wrong with me?

Have I lost it? Have I lost interest in spiritual things? Why does this routine seem so boring and so shallow?"

You find in the midst of *anywhere* that God is pouring out the Spirit. Everywhere you are, you find God. Think about this. God is anywhere, everywhere, because you are there. You do not have to go anywhere to find God. God is in you. You begin to have a realization of this, an awareness, a manifestation, as you journey.

When I went back to school, I went to an ordinary, secular, community college. As I walked down the halls, I would experience the most wonderful things. It was like angels were singing to me. I loved the feeling and I loved the wonderful people I met. They did not talk about the Lord. I did not talk about the Lord. But God was present to me there, and these people knew it, too. I did not have to tell them. To find out God is everywhere, and God can speak to you everywhere, is a great realization.

First, we experience unity when we come together in the banquet house, and there is some healing. Then God does this creative, healing work in us and starts sending us out. We find we are at home anywhere, and we are not so frightened. Jesus was not afraid. He did not hole up in the temple. He was out there with the people who needed him. We begin to notice: the Lord is here, the Lord is there, the Lord is in this Catholic, the Lord is in this Methodist. We begin to realize we have brothers and sisters in the Lord *everywhere*. They may not practice their faith the way we do, they may not use the same kind of language, but they nonetheless are growing in their own journey. I am one with them in the Spirit.

We notice something else, too. We notice we have brothers and sisters everywhere by virtue of creation. God has created so many people, and every person walking the face of this earth is God's creation. Each one has been created with a body, soul and spirit. Maybe their spirit has a big empty hole in it, but they are on a journey, just like I am on a journey.

Something happens inside of us when we see these people and realize, "This is my brother, this is my sister. Maybe they have not found God, but it does not make them any less my brother or my sister." God wants us to see this; to love each person because they are God's creation. God loves them. Christ died for them.

As we seek God's face, as we put ourselves in a position to let God do this creative work in us, we begin to recognize our brothers and sisters. Through Christ, God reconciled the world. Through us, God is reconciling the world. Every person becomes our brother or our sister. All are seekers, all are struggling, all are on this journey. God sends us out to love them from unreality to reality, to love them enough to give them space to become.

First it is myself, then it is myself and God, then myself and the Church, then myself and society, then myself and the world. We open up. Part of opening up is opening our eyes. We begin to really look around, to get out of our cloister and *see*. We need to meditate not only on our life circumstances, but also on world events, on the morning paper and the 6 o'clock news. We need to see what God is saying beyond us, in the world. We can't live in a box; we need to lift up our heads and take a look.

Maybe this does not sound very "spiritual." What does this have to do with prayer? It has a lot to do with prayer. We need to see beyond nationalism. We treat nationalism as if it is Christian, as if part of being a Christian is also being a patriot. Maybe it is to a degree; we have to work for the national well-being and pray for our leaders so we can live a Godly and peaceable life.

But our world is a big place. In every country on this earth we have brothers and sisters: in Bangladesh, in Russia, in Germany, in Poland, in Africa. In all these countries, we have fellow believers. When we lift a missile up and aim it, we are aiming it at our own people. We need to think about this, meditate about it, pray about it.

We need to pray, to ask God to show us how we are to live in the world community. We need to think about the fact that all people on the face of this earth are our brothers and our sisters and our responsibility, too: to love and care for, to feed and clothe, to assist in whatever way we can.

We need to open our eyes and see, we need to know how to pray. We need to take the blinders off our eyes. We need to pray for our government and for our leaders. We need to pray for the disadvantaged, for the poor in the world. Scripture tells us to feed and clothe the poor; we need to do this. It does not say to arm the poor, but it does say to feed and clothe them. In some simplistic way maybe we can do something on our level. Can we buy products that come from people directly? Can we go to the market right here and buy from the person who grows, so the farmer gets the money instead of the twelve people in between?

It is simplistic of us to think evangelism is only going out and handing out tracts. It is more than going out and winning somebody. It is also helping them learn to feed themselves. It is also planting a crop for the future. In Ghana, the Youth with a Mission people are farming. They share the Gospel while teaching them how to grow beans. This is evangelism! As we grow in the Lord, our heart opens up to everyone, and everyone's burdens. We need to be there, to love, caring enough to be with them as Jesus did. Jesus did not sit in the temple and send stuff out to the lepers. He went out among them.

Mother Teresa was a wonderful icon for us. But there is also somebody else we need to remember. We need to remember the woman who continually interceded in prayer for Mother Teresa. Mother Teresa depended much on intercession. The woman praying was present in India as much as was Mother Teresa. Maybe our role is to intercede.

I met a man in Tanzania. His name is Dave Simonson. He has been there for thirty-some years as a missionary, along with his wife, Eunie. They work with the Masai, people who wear robes, carry spears, raise cattle. They are nomadic. The Simonsons have lived with these people for about 37 years. The Masai have made Dave an elder of the tribe. He is the only outsider they have ever honored. He has started hundreds of schools in the area. Can you imagine that?—hundreds of schools started by one person! And his wife . . . half the town calls her "Mama." They come to her door day and night for medical help. Many of the young people in the town have been delivered by Mama; she delivers babies for these women. God, through Christ, was reconciling the world. God wants to be in us making a difference. We cannot all go to Tanzania, but we can all live in such a way as to make a difference.

We need to love enough to be hands-on, whether it is Tanzania or right here on the streets. We need to be where the need is, to be able to love people. But we cannot all actually go out. Therese of Lisieux said, "God, I want to be a missionary. God, I want to be a priest. God, I want to be . . . How can I?"

She was cloistered in a little place in France. She discovered her vocation was love, and she was a missionary, she was a priest because she prayed for people. In her heart she carried them to the throne of grace every day, and she lived her cloistered life in sacrificial love on their behalf.

Do we believe in the power of prayer? We can be in Bangladesh, Russia, Germany, Poland or Africa in prayer, if not in reality. We can allow God entrance into our lives so we can be freed of our unreal self and become the image of Christ. We can allow Christ to be formed in us. We can give ourselves fully to God on behalf of those for whom we pray. It makes a difference.

When we enter into this kind of self-sacrifice, or self-giving, we have no idea what the end is going to be. We do not know where it will take us. But we do not need to know the end. Our role is to give ourselves. Our role is to be open to God, to let Christ be formed in us. We can do it on behalf of those we know are in need, on behalf of the world. I can open myself in such a way. I can yearn, and I can long for God's will to be done on earth. I can ask God to transform me. I can be what God wants. I can feel what God feels. I can will what God wills. I can carry the burden God carries. I can suffer on behalf of those for whom God suffers. I can feel with God's heart and see with God's eyes.

The consecrated life of prayer, the self-giving in prayer on behalf of those in need, is probably the most powerful of intercessions. Will it make a difference if some farmer in North Dakota is living in obedience to Christ, loving God and being what God asks him to be, praying as God asks him to pray, loving God fully on behalf of the world? Will it make a difference? Did it make a difference that a poor carpenter walked around a little town in the Middle East being fully obedient to God, even to laying down his life? Did it make a difference? Will it make a difference? *"As the Father has sent me, so I send you."* It will make a difference if we consecrate ourselves so others might be consecrated. If we give ourselves fully, if we care for others and love them, if we treat them as brothers and sisters, if we are willing to lay down our lives for them. It makes a difference. Our yearning, our agony, our tears will make a difference. We may never see it, but nonetheless, it has effect.

We probably cannot go to Tanzania, but we can give ourselves to God. We can allow God to transform us into the image of Jesus, so God can be in us reconciling the world.

Scriptures for Meditation:
John 17:15-19,
John 20:21-22,
Matthew 9:36-38,
Acts 10:9-16; 17:16-31; 19:11-12,
Isaiah 6:1-8.

Lord, transform us into your likeness that we might live fully consecrated to you. Lord, enable us to live for your sake and that of the world. May you be glorified on earth, as you are in heaven, through us.

O holy and gracious God, I pray you would refresh us, you would come and clear away the drowsiness and, Lord, open us up as though we were brand new and fresh, as though we have just begun. Open us up to hear a fresh word, to allow you to stir our hearts. Creator, make us hunger and a thirst for you, that we would be so earnest that our desire for you would be unquenchable, that you would place in us such a desire that our whole life could be lived in quest of the full vision of who you are. And then, the day you call us home, we will cross over into the eternal vision and we will know you because we have been with you every moment and every day of our lives. God, only you can give us the gift of desire and we pray you would do so. We present ourselves to you, do in us what you will. Amen

We Are Called

We began talking about a journey, a journey of transformation, of God changing us into the image of Christ. We began by saying this journey is not something brand new, but that we were originally created to be in God's image. Through our brokenness, we fell from what we were intended to be. Jesus comes to redeem us and to recreate in us God's original intention.

But all God's immensity cannot be contained in one little picture, or in one person. God becomes manifest in each of us through this earthen vessel. God becomes manifest in a very unique and creative way. We are to be like Christ, fully human and yet filled with divine life, manifesting divine life through this particular vessel, with this particular color of hair, this particular manner of talking and this particular personality. Jesus has a unique Sonship. We know none of us will ever be Christ, but scripture says *we can be like Christ,* we can be his brothers and sisters. Jesus is the firstborn, the first one.

Sometimes, in our families, it seems that everyone comes from the same mold. We may even look alike. But our personalities are different and unique. We may wonder, "How did we all end up to be so different, coming out of the same mold, coming out of the same two people, out of the same family environment? How did we end up being so different from one another?"

As a parent, I want my children to become who they are, not who I am, or who my husband is, or who the Church thinks they should or shouldn't be. I want my children to become who they are created to be, because it is the only way they are really going to be happy, from a very natural standpoint. There are certain important characteristics I hope for, certain foundational things, but their expression can be different in each child. This is true with God as well, with God, our heavenly parent. God is calling us forth to become. We all share the same basic foundational things in our union with God. We are part of the Body of Christ, we have the indwelling Christ within us, we have the Holy Spirit within us, and God wants to live life in and through us.

There is not, however, a prescribed form somebody has determined for a Christian. The expression is who God created *us* to be. As God lives life in and through *us*, it will shine out—the light out of this particular earthen vessel. This is why it is so important to allow God to heal us and to do the interior work of removing walls and barriers, and lies, so we can allow the unique person God has created us to be to come forth.

God is saying, "Come out, Joann! Come out, Nancy! Come out, Renee! Come out! Don't be afraid, because I've created you. You are mine, chosen and precious." This is what God wanted: a Renee, a Nancy, a Joann. God knew it, even before we were born. Our whole life journey is one of coming out and *becoming*.

We are never fully out, never fully who God has created us to be. But moment by moment, God is freeing us. God is freeing us of all the walls and barriers and lies. But it has to happen within. It is not something somebody can apply on top of you.

This is why we need to dwell in God's presence, because God knows us, *God* changes us. Most of the change comes without our even knowing it, when we allow God to become manifest within us, when we sit at God's feet and bask in the sunlight of God's presence.

When we allow Love to pour into us and through us, God changes us. God wants this reality, this real person.

Experiencing God's presence will change our whole life, our communion with God, our prayer. Our relationship with God will come first. We will understand that everything else comes out of this relationship, instead of trying to fit everything else in first. It will not be a Christian "duty" to pray. Our life of prayer will become every communion, every touch, and every interaction with God.

We can live in prayer all day long. We can have times alone, set times, but we can also live in prayer. We can be turning to God all day long, turning to God's presence moment by moment, so that God has entrance into our lives. We can be living a life of prayer, a life with God, giving God entrance all the time. God is there. Our turning is simply to God who is already present, so we can allow necessary changes. Jesus said in John 17:19, *"And for their sakes I sanctify myself, so that they also may be sanctified in truth."*

We have to go back to the beginning and say, "I am willing to give myself to you, to allow you full entrance into my life. I want to live in your presence, and bask in your presence, and allow you to *create* me." Even if I myself do not want to be sanctified (but how could I not?) I must do it for *their* sake. The world needs me to become me. My family needs me to become me. The Church needs me to become me. I might be a voice, a hand, a foot or an arm missing in the Kingdom. If I am out limping along wounded and introverted, into my own woundedness and brokenness, I might be a vital missing part of the Kingdom. But if I allow God to set me free to become myself (the one God is creating me to be) maybe I can be the elbow or the finger, the vital piece God created me to be.

Frank Laubach writes,

> "Is God your friend, or do you love God? It is this stage that is really vital. How is it to be achieved? Precisely as any friendship is achieved, by doing things together. The depth and intensity of this friendship will depend on the variety and extent of the things we do and enjoy together. Will the friendship be constant? That again depends upon the permanence of our common interests and upon whether or not our interests grow into ever widening circles so that we do not stagnate. The highest friendship demands growth, it must be progressive as life itself is progressive. Friends must walk together; they cannot long stand still together, for that means death to the friendship and to life. Friendship with God is the friendship of child with parent. As an ideal son grows daily into a closer relationship with his father, so we may grow into closer love with God by widening into His interests and thinking His thoughts, and sharing His enterprises."

Moment by moment, we are allowing God entrance. Remember Moses' face shone with the radiance of God? Moses did not even know he was radiant. The people had to tell him. The radiance came from being with God, speaking face to face, and Moses was changed into that glorious likeness. It is the same with us; it is not by our effort, but by being with God we are changed.

Laubach goes on to say,

> "It is our duty to live in the beauty of the presence of God on some mount of

> transfiguration until we become white with Christ. After all, the deepest truth is that the Christ-like life is glorious, undefeatably glorious. Oh, if we would only let God have His full chance, He will break our heart with the glory of His revelation. It is my business to look into the very face of God until I ache with bliss."

Even if we never think about evangelism, isn't this enough reason to enter God's presence? The world is waiting for us to come forth. We can think of the Church as people coming forth, coming forth, coming forth, and each one coming out unique, unique, unique. How beautiful. The Church is like a field of many different kinds of flowers. Have you ever seen pictures of a mountainside full of wild flowers, an array of color, of beauty, all different? *They grow wild.*

This is the way the Church needs to become, all these beautiful creations becoming their own color, their own person—each one coming forth. The world is waiting for this to happen. The world looks at the Church and sees fragmentation, infighting, disputes, and criticism, instead of seeing unity and love. God would have us come forth and become the people of God we were created to be. God has no other bodies, the Holy Spirit has no vessels, we are the Temple. If the Church is going to *become*, it has to *become* through us. Jesus is not abstract. He lives through us and he is contemporary and he is living now. The world is waiting for him. We need to let Jesus heal us of the unreality of our broken self, so that we can become the reality of who God is creating us to be: our true self.

Scriptures for Meditation:
Exodus 33:11-23
John 15:15
John 14:16-21
Matthew 11:27-30

Lord, bring us into your Present Reality. May we abide in union with you and reflect your glory.

The Lord bless you and keep you;
The Lord make his face shine upon you,
And be gracious to you;
The Lord lift up his countenance upon you,
And give you peace.

Order Form

Please send _______copies of

Journey Into Reality
to:

____

Name

____

Address

____

City State Zip

Use this order form or give equivalent information and send to:

LIVING WATERS PUBLISHING
15590 Highland Avenue N.W.
Prior Lake, MN 55372
Toll-free # 888-950-2772

Be sure to include:
Check or money order for $9.95, and 6.5% Sales Tax (only if shipped to a Minnesota address).

(We are able to give discounts if ordering more than one copy. Please call for our discount schedule.)

Other books by Living Waters Publishing:

Journey from Self to God by Joann Nesser - *$4.50*
Love's Face by Margaret Montreuil - *$11.00*
Writing from the Fire Within by Margaret Montreuil - *$4.50*

Excerpts can be read on our web page:
http://www.livingwaterspublishing.com